Barfbag Origami

 Fly the queasy skies!

Twenty-Seven First-Class Gags to Get Your Creative Juices Flowing

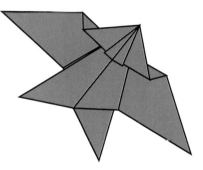

Chris **Marks**

The Lyons Press
Guilford, Connecticut
An imprint of The Globe Pequot Press

To buy books in quantity for corporate use
or incentives, call **(800) 962-0973**
or e-mail **premiums@GlobePequot.com.**

The Lyons Press is an imprint of The Globe Pequot Press.

This book was conceived, designed, and produced by
Paperwasp, an imprint of Balley Design Limited,
The Mews, 11 Wilbury Grove,
Hove, East Sussex, UK, BN3 3JQ
www.paperwaspbooks.com

Creative director: Simon Balley
Author: Chris Marks
Project editor: Sophie Collins
Designer: Tonwen Jones
Illustrations: Rob Brandt

Library of Congress Cataloging-in-Publication Data is available on file.
ISBN 978-1-59921-563-1
Printed in China
10 9 8 7 6 5 4 3 2 1

Contents

Introduction

These days, there isn't much to be said for flying as entertainment. Any unorthodox behavior will earn you a forcible detention and, should you decide to employ these surplus hours in practicing your craft skills, you'll find yourself severely limited in the materials you can bring on board. Welcome to barfbag origami.

Employ your new skills with caution and care. Involve those around you in the fun and give plenty of warning before launching. If you are trying out any origami flyers always be very careful NOT to hit anyone or to throw anything where it can cause damage or annoyance (your neighbor won't enjoy a barfbag plane, however beautifully made, landing in his or her in-flight meal).

When you try out the models in *Barfbag Origami* use your imagination and experiment to see what new types of flying objects you can design. No two airplanes ever fly the same, so don't be disheartened if yours does not fly the first time around. Don't worry if you have problems with your initial attempts. Revisit the instructions and check the illustrations in sequence. At each step, look at the next illustration to see what shape your paper should make as the result of the step you are following. Also remember that the arrows show the direction in which the paper has to be folded. So look very carefully to see which way the arrows go over, through, and under, and fold your paper accordingly. To help you become accomplished at barfbag origami, here are some tips:

>> Fold on a flat surface, such as your airplane tray table, or a book.

>> Make your folds neat and accurate. Crease your folds into place by running your thumbnail along them.

>> In the illustrations, the shading represents the printed side of the barfbag.

>> If your airplane doesn't fly the first time around, make sure that it is not bent out of shape or wrinkled in any way.

>> If your origami project isn't working, take some time out. Place your flying object to one side, go for a walk up and down the plane's aisles, have a cup of coffee, or chat with an in-flight attendant. Once you are calm, try making a new creation.

>> Using only the in-flight barfbag and this manual, you can create any number of paper flying machines. Don't worry about running out of raw material — your neighbors, impressed by your skills, are certain to rush to get their own barfbags converted into an amazing aerodrome of super flyers.

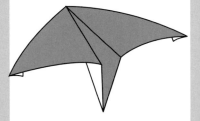

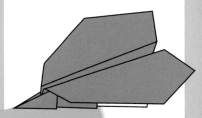

I do hope that you have a great deal of fun and enjoyment with Barfbag Origami.

Happy flying!

Chris Marks

Operational Symbols

The following symbols help explain how these projects are constructed. Make sure that you understand the differences between each fold. If you get them mixed up, there are no guarantees as to what kind of flight patterns your flying objects will take off on!

A valley fold (fold toward you, or in front) is indicated by a line of dashes and a solid arrow showing the direction in which the paper has to be folded.

A mountain fold (fold backward, or behind) is indicated by a line of dots and dashes and a hollow-headed arrow showing the direction in which the paper has to be folded.

A solid black line indicates to tear the paper in the direction shown.

An arrow which comes back on itself indicates to fold, press flat, and unfold the paper back to its previous position.

A looped arrow indicates to turn the paper over in the direction shown.

Two circling arrows indicates to turn the paper around into the position shown.

A hollow arrow with a short indented tail indicates to open, and press the paper down flat into the position shown in the next illustration.

A solid headed arrow indicates to push the paper in along the fold-lines, as shown.

A swollen arrow with a pointed tail indicates that the illustration alongside is drawn to a larger scale.

A line with a Z-shape in the middle indicates that there's more paper beyond this point, but it has not been drawn.

Shaping Your Barfbag

Airlines have been slow to see the alternative possibilities in the standard barfbag format, so you will have to tailor your material to create the perfect origami square or rectangle. You won't be able to use scissors to cut the paper, so practice folding and tearing accurately and precisely along the fold-lines.

Before you begin, gently pull apart your barfbag along its glued seam and bottom folded section, opening it out completely.

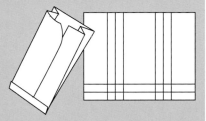

Many of the projects that follow begin with a square. Here's a quick and easy way to make one:

1 Place the opened-out barfbag on a flat surface, sideways on, with the plain side on top. Valley fold the left-hand side down to meet the bottom edge, making a triangle with a rectangular strip of paper adjacent to it.

2 Valley fold the rectangular strip over the triangle's right-hand side, as shown. Press flat and unfold it. Repeat this step a few more times, thereby weakening the paper slightly.

3 Carefully tear along the fold-line made in step 2.

4 To complete, open out the triangle into a square. Put the strip of paper aside—it can be used in another project.

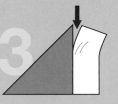

 **1**

The Straight Arrow

Difficulty

Neat, uncomplicated, and with absolutely no vices, this simple little plane is a joy to fold, even in a thunderstorm. Make it to steady your nerves!

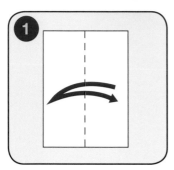

1 Place the opened-out barfbag lengthways, plain side up. Fold it in half vertically, then unfold.

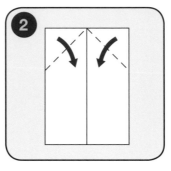

2 Valley fold the top corners down to meet the middle fold-line.

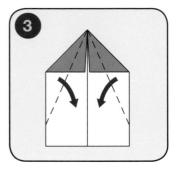

3 From the top point, valley fold the sloping edges in to meet the middle fold-line.

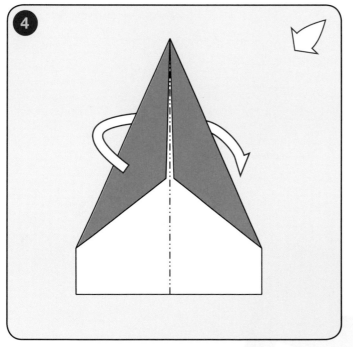

4 Mountain fold the paper in half from left to right.

5 From the top point, valley fold the front flap of paper in half from right to left, making a wing.

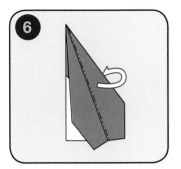

Repeat step 5 with the back flap, mountain folding it behind to make the second wing.

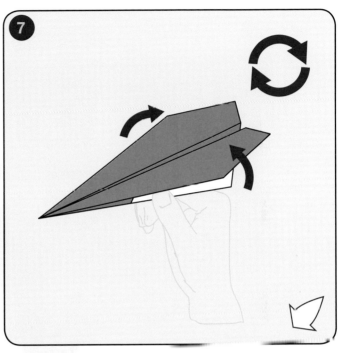

To complete, lift the wings up, so that they are at right angles to the body. To fly, hold the Straight Arrow between the thumb and forefinger and launch it gently forward.

The Aerofoil

2

Difficulty

This extremely simple flying object takes only a few seconds to fold. It will travel surprisingly fast through the air, losing height slowly as it glides.

1

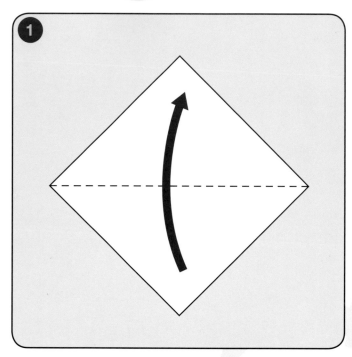

Tear your barfbag into a square. Place it plain side up, and turn it so that one corner is toward you. Valley fold it in half from bottom to top, to make a triangle.

2

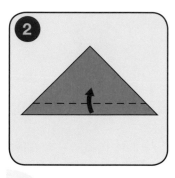

Valley fold the triangle's bottom edge up.

3

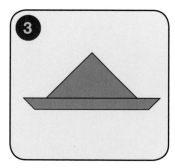

You will now have a small band of paper along the bottom edge.

4

Turn the paper over. Bring the band's ends to meet one another.

5

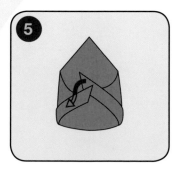

Tuck one end deep into the other, making a tube-like shape.

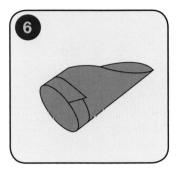

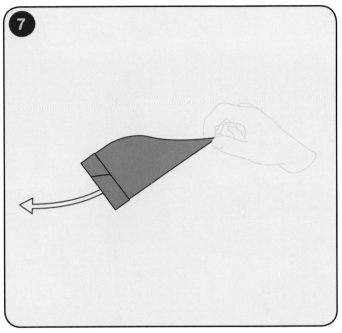

To complete, curve the paper slightly with your hands to make your Aerofoil as even and round as possible.

To fly, hold the Aerofoil by its tip between the thumb and forefinger and launch it with a gentle push forward.

The Snub-nosed Jet

3

Difficulty

This flying object is a long range glider. With its large wings and weighty nose, it should zoom a long way. Special care should be taken to avoid a direct hit.

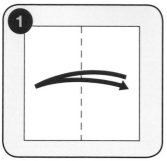

1 Start with a square, plain side up. Fold it in half vertically, then unfold.

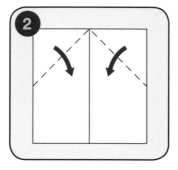

2 Valley fold the top corners down to meet the middle fold-line.

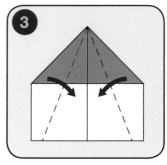

3 From the top point, valley fold the sloping edges in to meet the middle fold-line.

4 Valley fold the top point down, as far as shown in the picture, leaving a blunt edge.

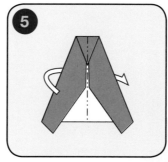

5 Mountain fold the paper in half from left to right.

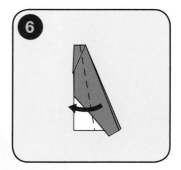

6 Valley fold the front flap of paper in half from right to left, making a wing.

7 Repeat step 6 with the back flap, mountain folding it behind to make the second wing.

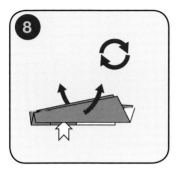

To complete, turn the paper around and lift the wings up, so that they are at right angles to the body.

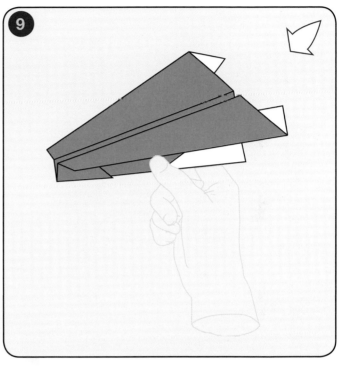

To fly, hold the Snub-nosed Jet between the thumb and forefinger and launch it gently forward.

 **4**

The Hang Glider

Be careful where you aim this glider: It's a distance flyer. Try a reciprocal arrangement with the passenger across the aisle to ensure a safe landing!

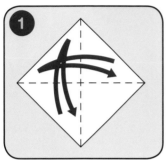

1 Start with a square, plain side up and one corner toward you. Fold and unfold it in half from corner to corner to mark the middle fold-lines.

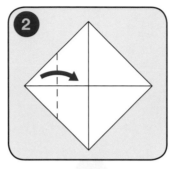

2 Valley fold the left-hand corner into the middle.

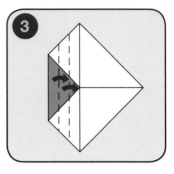

3 Valley fold the left-hand edge over one-third of the way to the middle, and then over again, as shown.

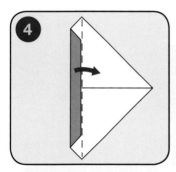

4 Valley fold the left-hand edge over along the adjacent vertical fold-line.

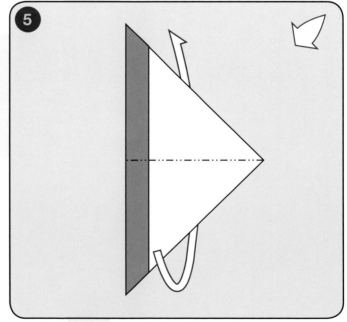

5 Mountain fold the paper in half from bottom to top.

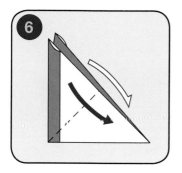

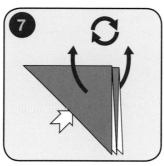

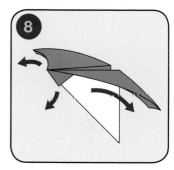

Valley fold the front flap of paper in half from top left to bottom right, making a wing. Repeat with the back flap to make the second wing.

Turn the paper around. Lift the wings up, so that they are at right angles to the body.

To complete, pull the front section of paper away from the model slightly, and gently bend each wing into a soft downward curve.

To fly, pinch the Hang Glider at its lower point between the thumb and forefinger and launch it with a gentle push forward.

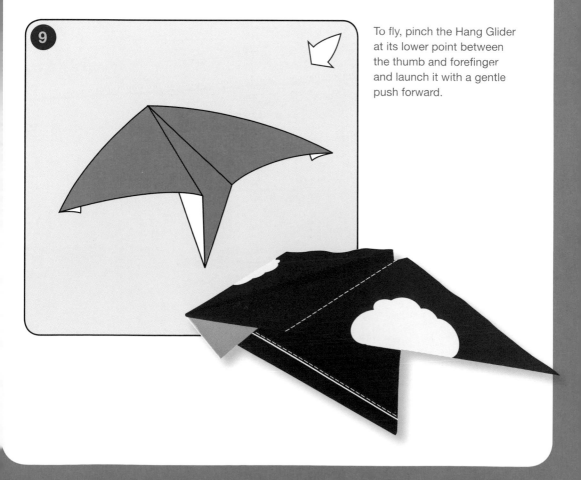

5

The Origami Plane

Difficulty

A traditional Japanese origami airplane with a simple—but clever—folded lock holding everything together. Use it to impress your fellow passengers!

Place the opened-out barfbag lengthways on, plain side up. Fold it in half vertically, then unfold.

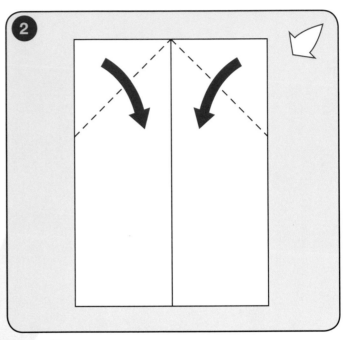

Valley fold the top corners down to meet the middle fold-line.

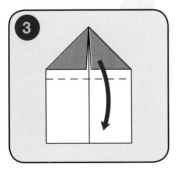

Valley fold the top point down to a point that is slightly short of the bottom edge.

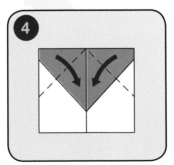

Again, valley fold the top corners down to meet the middle fold-line.

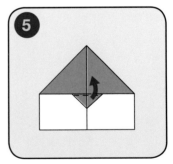

Valley fold the small triangle up over the adjacent edges. This will lock them together and prevent the model from unfolding itself during flight.

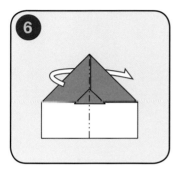

Mountain fold the paper in half from left to right.

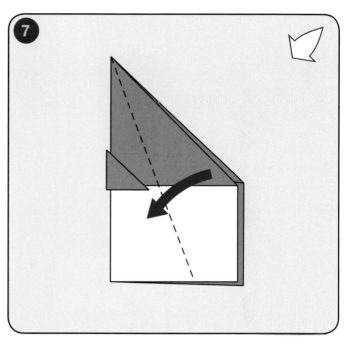

From the top point, valley fold the front flap of paper in half from right to left, making a wing.

Repeat step 7 with the back flap, mountain folding it behind to make the second wing.

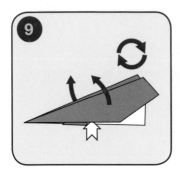

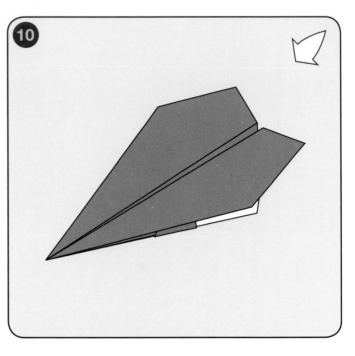

To complete the flyer, turn the paper around and lift the wings up, so that they are at right angles to the body.

To fly, hold the Origami Plane between the thumb and forefinger and launch it gently forward.

6

The Square Plane

Difficulty

This plane's large wing surface is great for writing on. Aim it carefully, so that your message reaches the intended recipient!

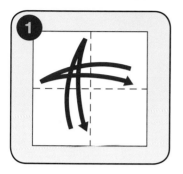

Start with a square, plain side up. Fold and unfold in half from side to side, and top to bottom.

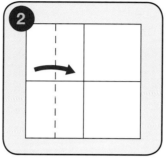

Valley fold the left-hand side in to the middle.

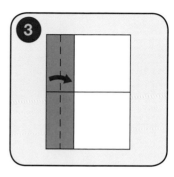

Valley fold the left-hand side over to meet the adjacent vertical fold-line.

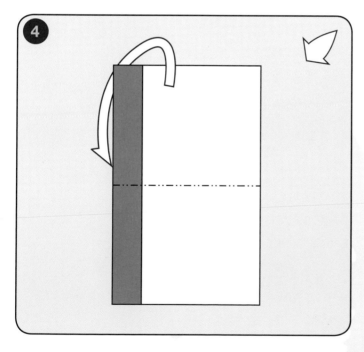

Mountain fold the paper in half from top to bottom.

6

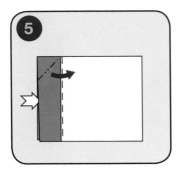

Lift the left-hand layers of paper up along the adjacent vertical fold-line. Insert your fingers in between the layers. Open them out.

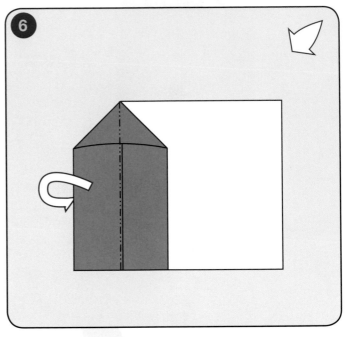

With your free hand, press their top down neatly into the shape of a triangular roof, to make the plane's nose. Mountain fold the remaining left-hand layer of paper behind, along the adjacent vertical fold-line.

Valley fold the front and back flaps up along a horizontal line that runs adjacent to the roof's bottom edge, making wings.

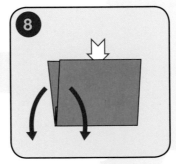

Fold the wings down, so that they are at right angles to the body.

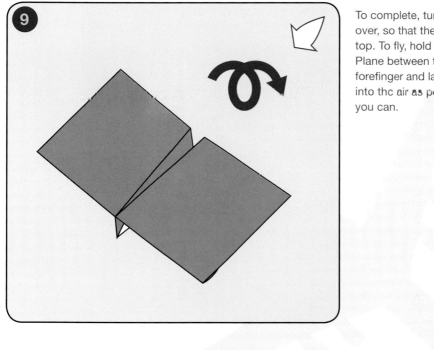

9

To complete, turn the paper over, so that the wings are on top. To fly, hold the Square Plane between the thumb and forefinger and launch it high into the air as powerfully as you can.

The Amazon Tumbler

7

Difficulty

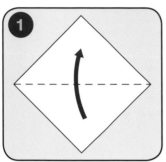

This wonderfully easy flyer turns somersaults as it gyrates through the air, just like a living butterfly. As always, fold neatly for a perfect result.

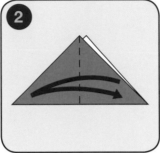

1

Start with a square, plain side up and one corner toward you. Valley fold it in half from bottom to top, making a triangle.

2

Fold and unfold the triangle in half from side to side.

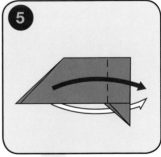

3

Treating them as if they were one, valley fold the triangle's two top points down, so that they overlap the bottom edge slightly.

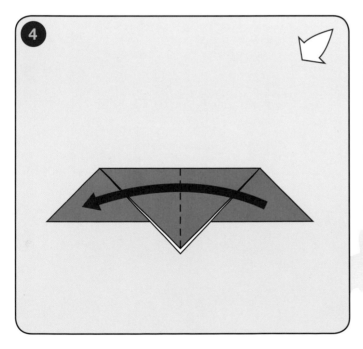

4

Valley fold the paper in half from right to left.

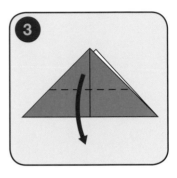

5

Valley fold the front left-hand flap of paper over to the right, as shown, making a wing. Repeat behind with the back flap to make the second wing.

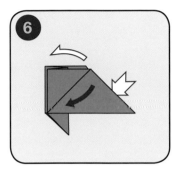

To complete, lift the wings up, so that they are at right angles to the body, and open out the two triangular pockets slightly.

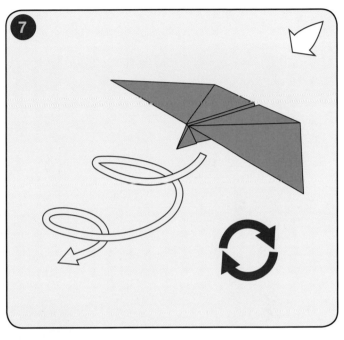

To fly, hold the Amazon Tumbler between the thumb and forefinger and launch it with a gentle push forwards.

The Sky Cruiser

Difficulty

This neat little plane is sturdy to fly, and will stand endless repeat performances. It's also simple to fold, so it's an ideal choice if you're accompanying a minor.

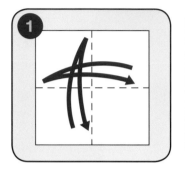

Start with a square, plain side up. Fold and unfold in half from side to side, and top to bottom.

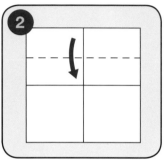

Valley fold the top edge in to the middle.

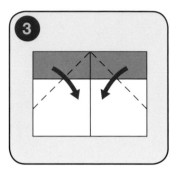

Valley fold the top corners down to meet the middle fold-line.

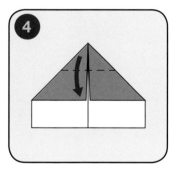

Valley fold the top point down to meet the adjacent horizontal edges and refold . . .

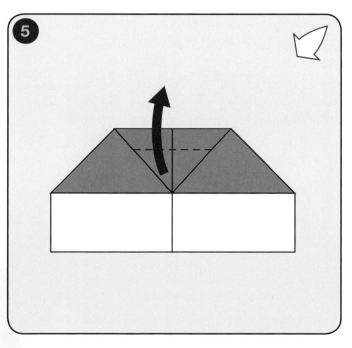

back up part of the way, so that it overlaps the top edge slightly.

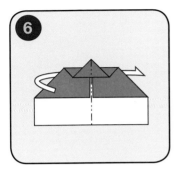

6

Mountain fold the paper in half
from left to right.

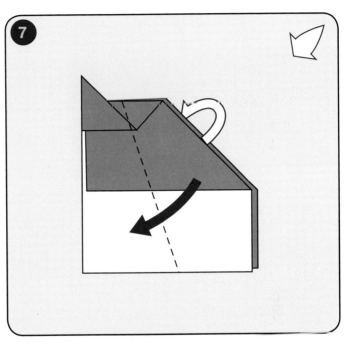

7

Valley fold the front flap of paper in half from right to left, making a
wing. Repeat behind with the back flap to make the second wing.

To attempt a record paper plane flight for
Guinness World Records, the flight distance
must be measured in a straight line. In
addition, the plane must roll no more than
four times in flight.

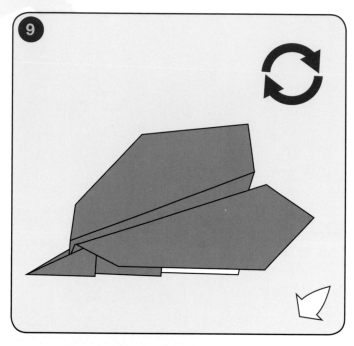

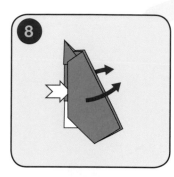

8

Lift the wings up, so that they are at right angles to the body.

9

To complete, turn the flyer around so that it's upright. To fly, hold the Sky Cruiser between the thumb and forefinger and launch it high into the air with as much force as possible.

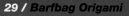

9

The Swift

Difficulty

This flyer is supposed to resemble a swift and, like its real-life counterpart, it has a fast, darting flight. Large wings and a heavy nose help it to cruise a long way.

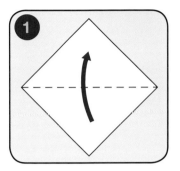

Start with a square, plain side up and one corner toward you. Valley fold it in half from bottom to top, to make a triangle.

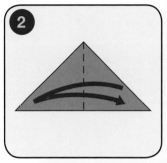

Fold and unfold the triangle in half from side to side.

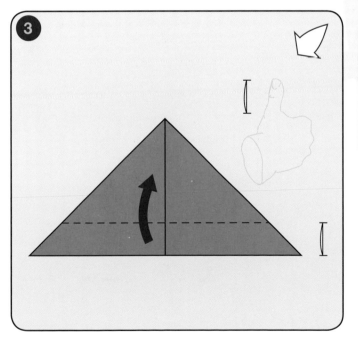

Valley fold the triangle's bottom edge up about two inches (about the length of your thumb), creating a band of paper at the base.

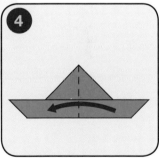

Valley fold the paper in half from right to left.

9

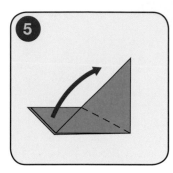

Valley fold the front flap of paper up on a line between the bottom right-hand corner and where the sloping and horizontal edges intersect, making a wing.

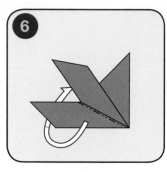

Repeat step 5 with the back flap, mountain folding it behind to make the second wing.

Turn the paper around. From the bottom right-hand corner, valley fold the front wing's right-hand sloping edge down to meet the bottom edge. Repeat behind with the back wing.

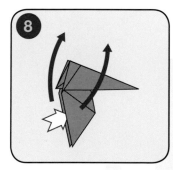

Lift the wings up, so that they are at right angles to the body.

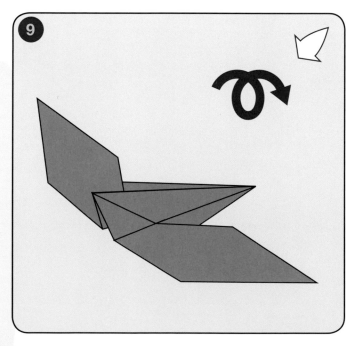

To complete, turn the flyer right side up. To fly, hold the Swift (from above) between thumb and forefinger and launch it firmly forward.

Paper planes have been recorded flying more than 190 feet. That's not much less than the length of the central aisle of the new Airbus A380.

 **10**

The Flying Squid

Resembling a squid "swimming" through the air, this plane is given super-stability by the small fins in front, making it one of the most interesting to fly.

Difficulty

Place the opened-out barfbag lengthways on, plain side up. Fold it in half vertically, then unfold.

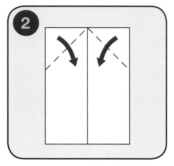

Valley fold the top corners down to . . .

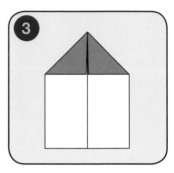

meet the middle fold-line.

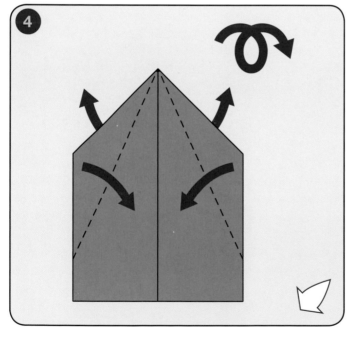

Turn the paper over. From the top point, valley fold the sloping edges in to meet the middle fold-line, at the same time letting the corners flick up from underneath.

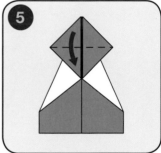

Valley fold the top point down on a line between the two side points.

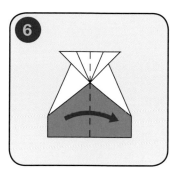

Valley fold the paper in half from left to right.

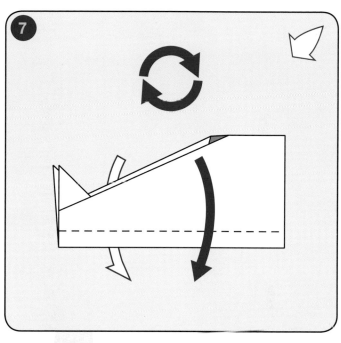

Turn the **paper around**. Valley fold the front flap of paper down, so that it **overlaps** the bottom edge, making a wing. Repeat **behind** with the back flap to make the second wing.

 From the 1910s through to the 1930s, paper planes were sometimes used by engineers to test the flight dynamics of real aircraft.

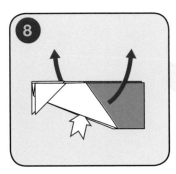

To complete the flyer, lift the wings up, so that they are at right angles to the body.

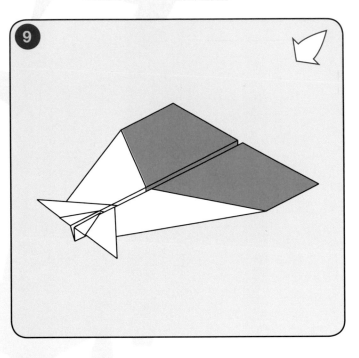

To fly, hold the Squid between the thumb and forefinger and launch it firmly forward.

11

The Swallow

Difficulty

One would never guess that this odd-looking design would fly, but the Swallow is a short-range glider and will scoot about perfectly in any kind of turbulence.

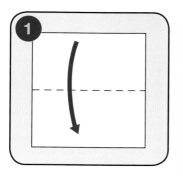

Start with a square, plain side up. Valley fold it in half from top to bottom.

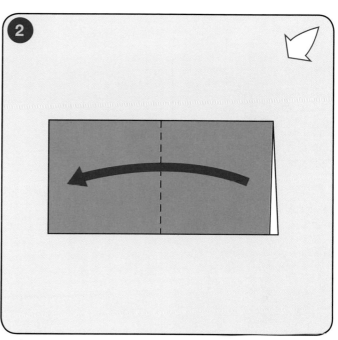

Valley fold the paper in half from right to left.

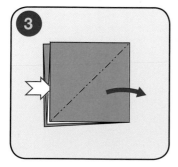

Lift the top half up along the middle fold-line. Open out the paper and . . .

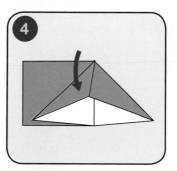

press it down neatly . . .

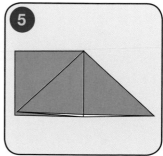

into a triangle.

11

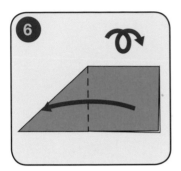

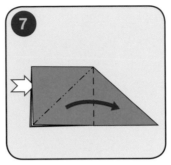

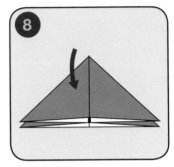

Turn the paper over. Valley fold in half from right to left.

Repeat steps 3 to 5 . . .

to make a shape known in origami as a waterbomb base.

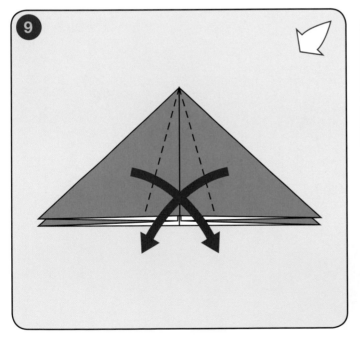

Valley fold the top point down to meet the middle of the bottom edge and refold . . .

From the top point, valley fold the right- and left-hand flaps of paper across the waterbomb base, so that they overlap each other, making the Swallow's V-shaped tail.

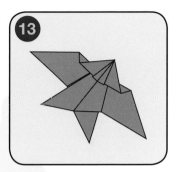

back up part of the way, so that it overlaps the top edge slightly.

To complete, valley fold the paper in half from right to left. Press it flat, unfold slightly, and bend each wing into a soft downward curve.

To fly, hold the Swallow by its tail between the thumb and forefinger and launch it with a gentle push forwards.

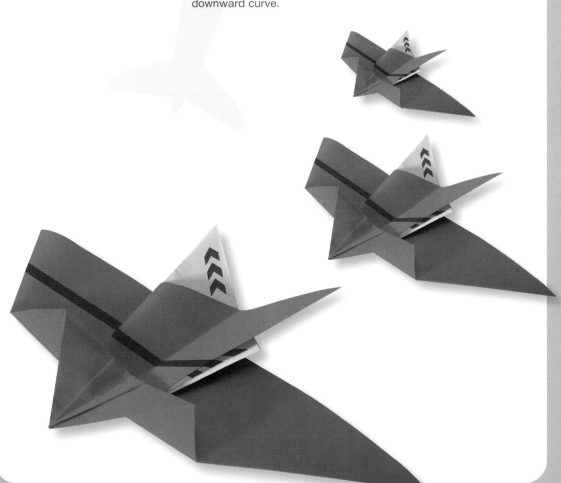

12 The Fly

Difficulty

An accomplished flying machine, the Fly is also strong and fast in flight. Take the time to make its folds crisp and sharp to get the best possible performance.

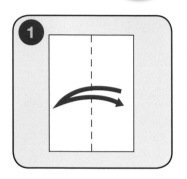

Place the opened-out barfbag lengthways, plain side up. Fold it in half vertically, then unfold.

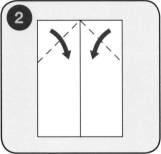

Valley fold the top corners down to meet the middle fold-line.

From the top point, valley fold the sloping edges in to meet the middle fold-line.

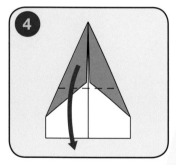

Valley fold the top point down, so that it overlaps the bottom edge slightly.

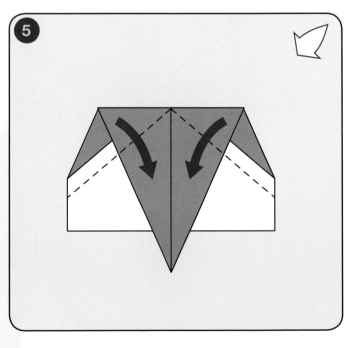

Valley fold the top corners down to meet the middle fold-line.

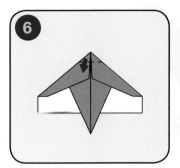

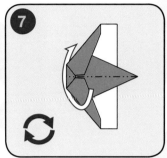

Valley fold the top point down just a little.

Turn the paper around. Mountain fold the paper in half from bottom to top.

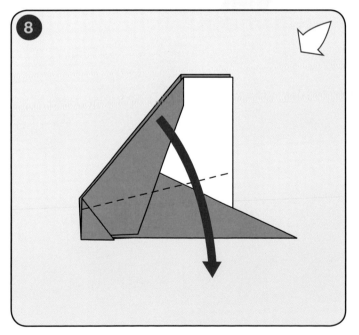

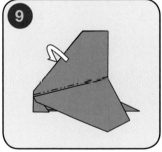

Repeat step 8 with the back flap, mountain folding it behind to make the second wing.

Valley fold the front flap of paper down on a slant, as shown, so that it overlaps the bottom edge slightly, making a wing.

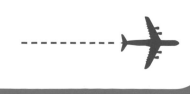

10

To complete, lift the wings up so that they are at right angles to the body.

11

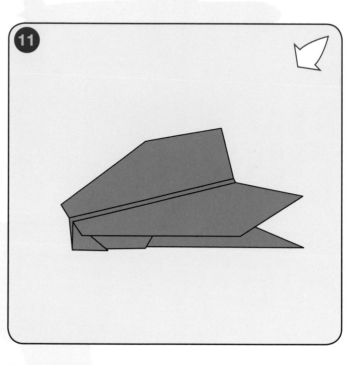

To fly, hold the Fly between the thumb and forefinger and launch it firmly forward.

13

The Futuristic Wing

Difficulty

Shaped like a triangle, this plane looks—and flies—like something out of the technological future. Very soon you will have it zipping in and out of the clouds.

1

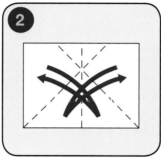

Place the opened-out barfbag sideways on, plain side up. Fold it in half vertically, then unfold.

2

Valley fold the sides down in turn to meet the bottom edge. Press flat, then unfold.

3

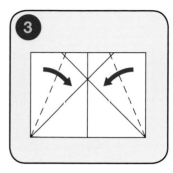

From the bottom right- and left-hand corners, valley fold the sides over to meet their adjacent sloping fold-lines.

4

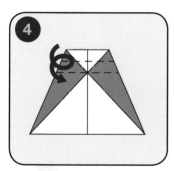

Valley fold the top edge down to where the folded-in corners meet, and then along a horizontal line running through them.

5

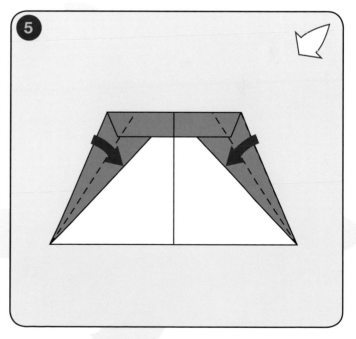

From the bottom right- and left-hand corners, valley fold the sides over to meet their adjacent sloping fold-lines.

13

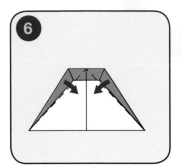

6

Starting in the middle of the top edge, valley fold the sides along their adjacent sloping fold-lines.

7

Mountain fold the paper in half from right to left.

8

Valley fold the bottom right-hand corner up on a slant, as shown. Press flat, then unfold.

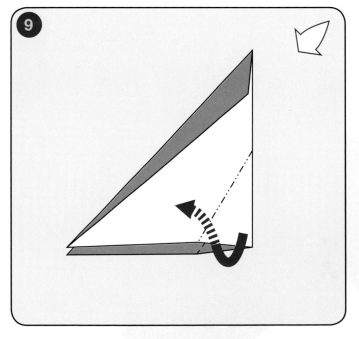

9

Using the fold-lines made in step 8 as a guide, push the corner up inside the model, making the plane's tail. Press it flat.

10

Valley fold the front flap of paper over to the right along a line that connects the model's top and bottom points, making a wing.

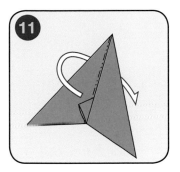

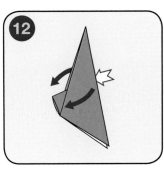

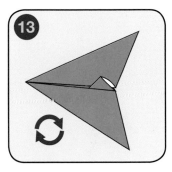

Repeat step 10 with the back flap, mountain folding it behind to make the second wing.

Lift the wings up, so that they are at right angles to the body.

Turn the paper around so that the plane is upright. To fly, hold the Futuristic Wing between the thumb and forefinger and launch it high into the air with a firm throw.

 **14**

The Chunky

Don't let the name of this plane put you off making it. As well as being very stable in flight, Chunky also travels for quite a long distance.

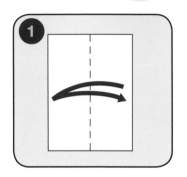

Place the opened-out barfbag lengthways on, plain side up. Fold it in half verically, then unfold.

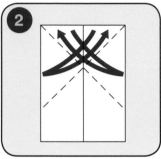

Valley fold the top edge over to lie along the right- and left-hand sides in turn. Press flat, then unfold.

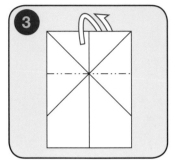

Mountain fold the top edge behind to meet the bottom of the diagonal fold-lines. Press flat, then unfold.

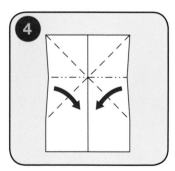

Press the middle of the fold-lines until the sides pop up. Using the fold-lines as a guide, bring the sides together and down toward you.

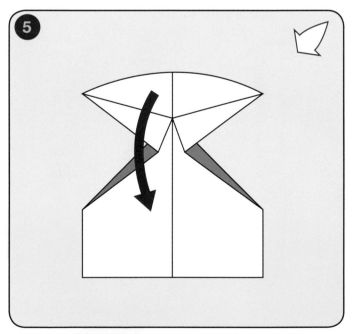

Press the top down neatly into a triangle, making a waterbomb base in one end of the paper.

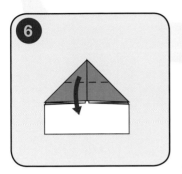

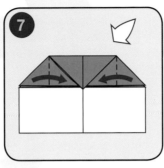

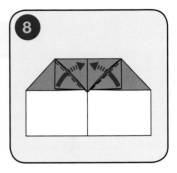

Valley fold the top point down, so that it overlaps the adjacent horizontal edges slightly.

Valley fold the bottom corner of each front flap over to meet the point's sloping edges, as shown.

Tuck the flaps into their adjacent pockets with a valley fold.

Valley fold the paper in half, from left to right.

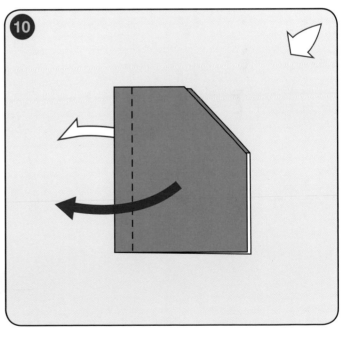

Valley fold the front flap of paper over, so that it overlaps the left-hand side, making a wing. Repeat behind with the back flap to make the second wing.

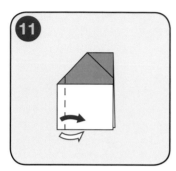

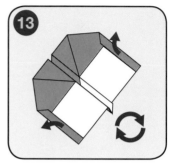

Valley fold the front wing's outer edge over toward the right slightly, to make a paper flap, or winglet. Repeat with the back wing.

Lift the wings up, so that they are at right angles to the body.

To complete, turn the paper around and stand the winglets upright, at right angles to the body.

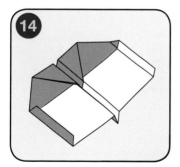

To fly, hold Chunky between the thumb and forefinger and launch it high into the air with a firm throw.

15

The Super Dart

Difficulty

When throwing this sleek flying machine, watch out for those around you: its pointed nose makes it a dangerous weapon if used without due caution!

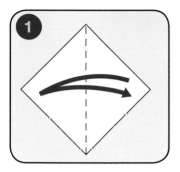

1 Start with a square, plain side up and one corner toward you. Valley fold it in half vertically, then unfold.

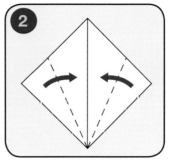

2 From the bottom corner, valley fold the sloping edges in to meet the middle fold-line, making a kite base.

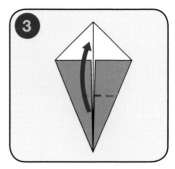

3 Valley fold the bottom point up, so that it overlaps the adjacent horizontal edges slightly.

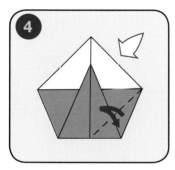

4 Valley fold the bottom right-hand corner over along a line between the middle of the bottom edge and the adjacent side point. Press flat, then unfold.

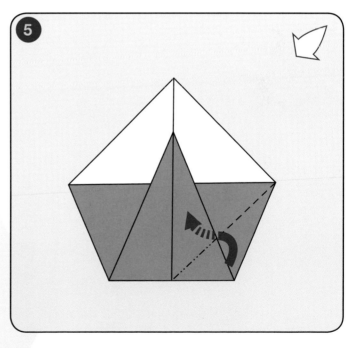

5 Using the fold-lines made in step 4 as a guide, push the bottom right-hand corner up inside the model. Press it flat.

15

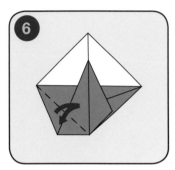

Repeat steps 4 and 5 with the bottom left-hand corner, making a diamond-shaped flap of paper.

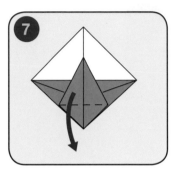

Valley fold the flap down along a horizontal line between its two side points.

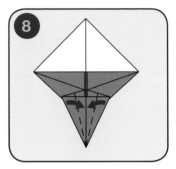

From the flap's bottom point, valley fold the sloping edges in to meet the middle fold-line, making the dart's pointed nose.

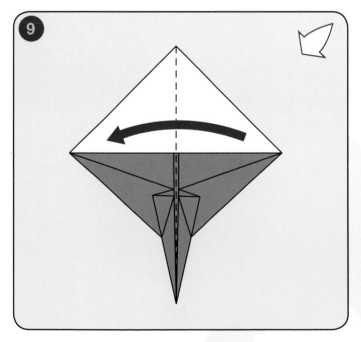

Valley fold the paper in half from right to left.

Turn the paper around. Following the top edge of the dart's pointed nose, valley fold the front flap of paper down, so that it overlaps the bottom edge, making a wing. Repeat behind with the back flap to make the second wing.

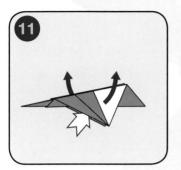

To complete, lift the wings up, so that they are at right angles to the body.

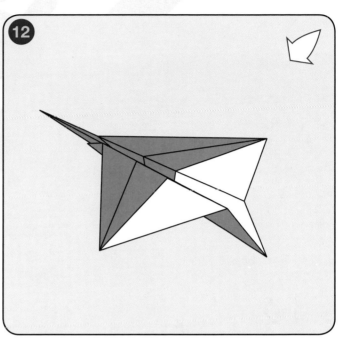

To fly, hold the Super Dart between the thumb and forefinger and launch it high into the air with a firm throw.

16   *The Bowtie*

Difficulty

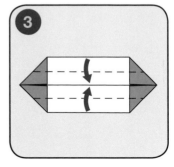

Amaze the cabin crew with this snazzy piece of flying attire. It's made from the little rectangle of paper left over when you shaped your barfbag into a square.

1

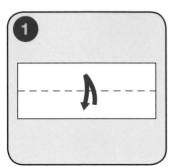

Place the paper sideways on, plain side up. Fold and unfold it in half from bottom to top.

2

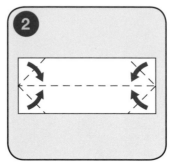

Valley fold the corners in to meet the middle fold-line.

3

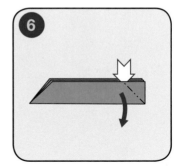

Valley fold the top and bottom edges in to meet the middle fold-line.

4

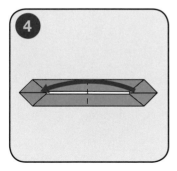

Valley fold the paper in half from right to left.

5

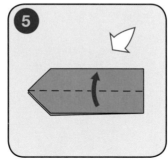

Valley fold the paper in half from bottom to top.

6

Insert your fingers in between the top layers of paper, as shown. Open them out, and with your free hand . . .

A tail isn't necessarily needed in a real plane—just like paper planes, some full-size craft have been designed (and have flown) without tails.

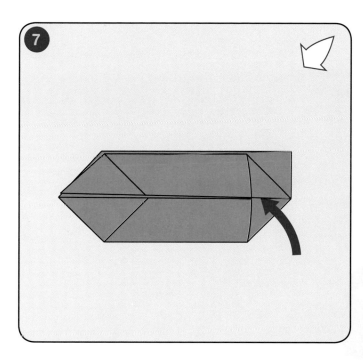

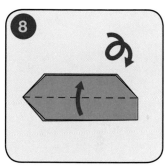

Turn the paper over from top to bottom. Repeat steps 6 and 7 with the bottom layers of paper.

press their sides down neatly into the shape of a triangular roof.

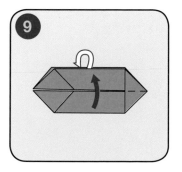

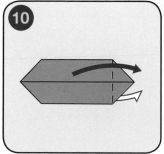

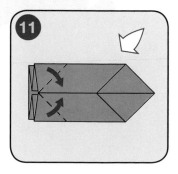

Valley fold one layer of paper in front and mountain fold one layer down behind, as though turning the pages of a book.

Valley fold the front flap of paper to the right on a line between the triangular roof's two side points. Repeat with the back flap by mountain folding it behind.

Valley fold the front left-hand corners in to meet the horizontal middle line.

16

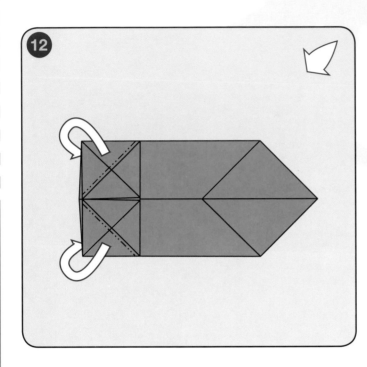

Repeat step 11 with the back left-hand corners by mountain folding them behind.

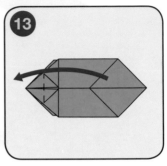

Valley fold the front flap of paper over to the left as far as it will comfortably go.

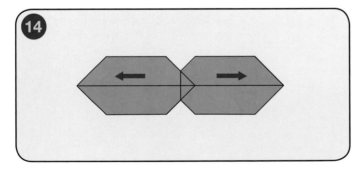

Take hold of a flap in each hand and gently pull them apart—in the process . . .

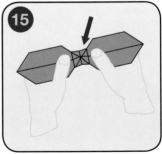

carefully flattening out the middle point. Press it flat. To complete, give the paper a soft mountain fold along its length.

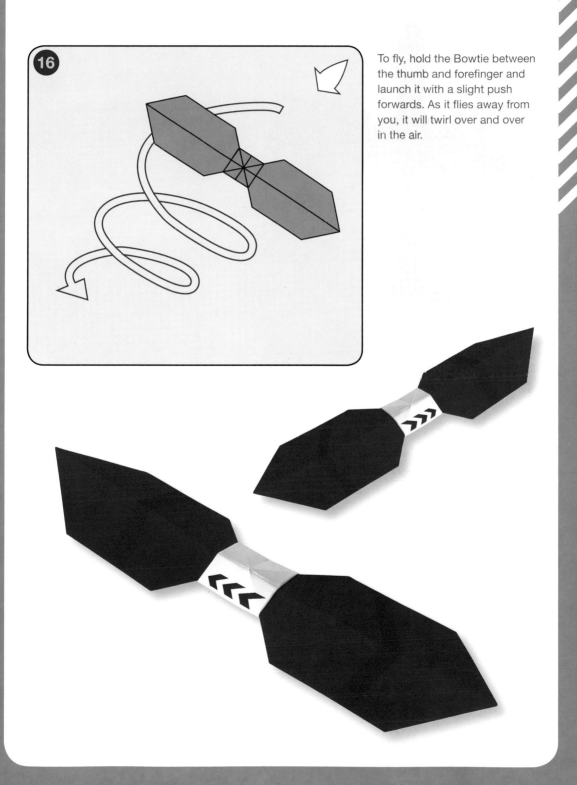

16

To fly, hold the Bowtie between the thumb and forefinger and launch it with a slight push forwards. As it flies away from you, it will twirl over and over in the air.

The Supersonic Jet

Difficulty

Why not try to break the sound barrier with this futuristic-looking jet? Make sure that you fold it neatly —even a small mistake will change the way it flies.

1

Start with a square, plain side up and one corner toward you. Fold and unfold it in half from corner to corner to mark the middle fold-lines.

2

Valley fold the top and bottom corners in to the middle.

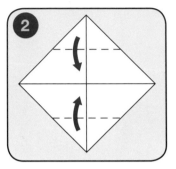

3

Valley fold the right- and left-hand halves of the top edge down to meet the middle fold-line.

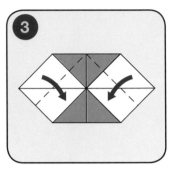

4

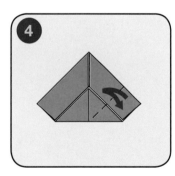

Valley fold the right-hand half of the bottom edge up to meet the middle fold-line. Press flat and unfold.

5

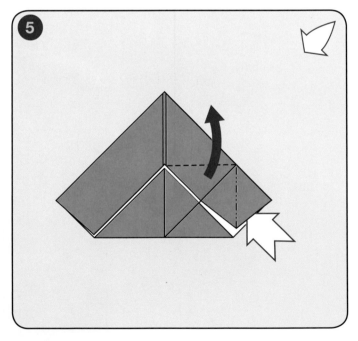

Reach inside and open out the layers of the right-hand side, making the horizontal valley fold as shown, at the same time . . .

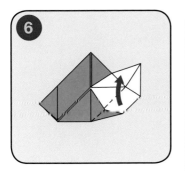

pushing its lower edge up along the valley fold-line made in step 4. Press the paper flat into a triangular pointed flap.

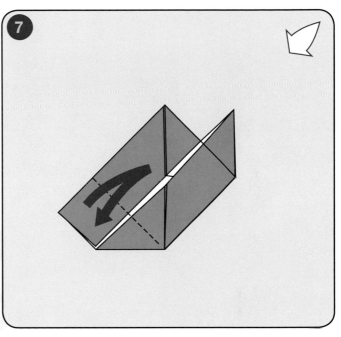

Repeat steps 4 to 6 with the left-hand half of the bottom edge and adjoining layers.

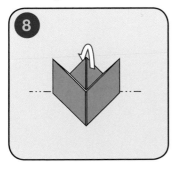

Mountain fold the middle point behind on a line between the two side points.

Valley fold the paper in half from right to left.

Turn the paper round. Valley fold the front flap of paper down, so that it overlaps the bottom edge slightly, making a wing.

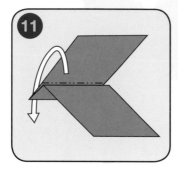

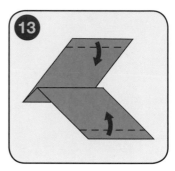

Repeat step 10 with the back flap, mountain folding it behind to make the second wing.

Lift the wings up, so that they are at right angles to the body.

To complete, valley fold the outer edge of each wing upright, making the winglets.

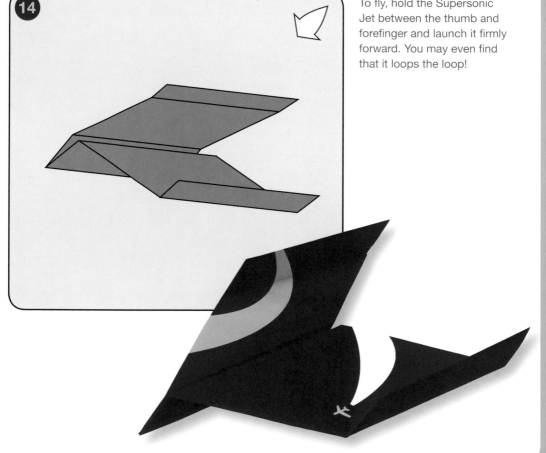

To fly, hold the Supersonic Jet between the thumb and forefinger and launch it firmly forward. You may even find that it loops the loop!

 **18**

The Flapping Bird

Difficulty

This ingenious design will flap its wings majestically between your fingers, just like a real bird.

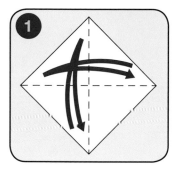

Start with a square, plain side up and one corner toward you. Fold and unfold it in half from corner to corner to mark the middle fold-lines.

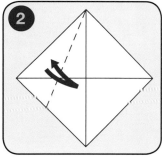

From the top corner, valley fold the left-hand sloping edge in to meet the middle fold-line. Press flat and unfold.

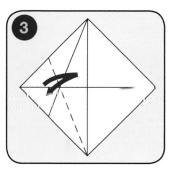

From the bottom corner, valley fold the left-hand sloping edge in to meet the middle fold-line. Press flat and unfold.

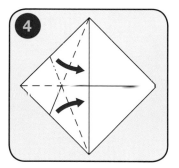

Using the fold-lines made in steps 2 and 3 as a guide, pinch together the sloping edges and fold . . .

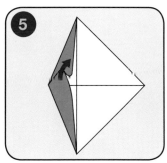

the triangular flap, that appears as you pinch, upward.

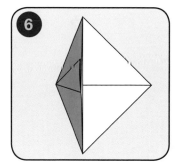

Press the paper flat to complete an origami technique known as a "rabbit's ear."

Turn the paper over. Repeat steps 2 to 6.

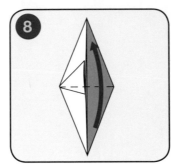

Valley fold the paper in half from bottom to top.

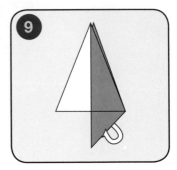

Bring the right-hand triangular flap around from behind the model, making it point downward in the process.

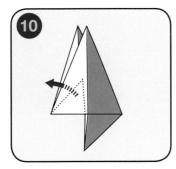

From in between the left-hand layers of paper, pull out the hidden triangular flap. Press it down neatly into the position shown in step 11.

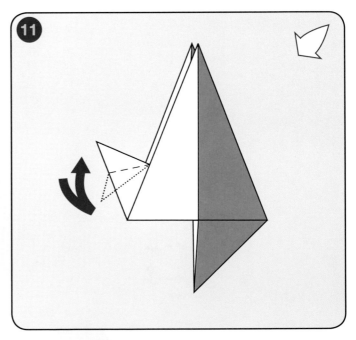

Valley fold a little of the flap's tip over on a slant. Press flat and unfold.

To complete, turn the flap's tip inside out, using the fold-lines made in step 11 as a guide. This makes the bird's head. Press it down neatly into the position, as shown in step 13.

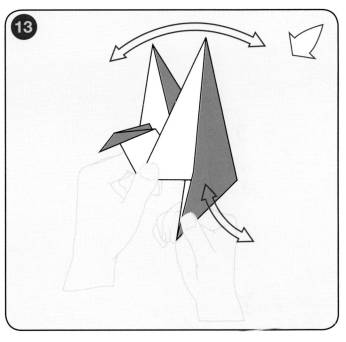

To make the wings flap, hold its chest with one hand and pull the tail gently back and forth with the other.

19 The Bat

Difficulty

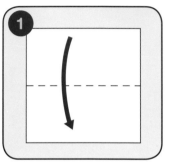

Fly this creature during the darkness of an in-flight horror movie and you might find that it's mistaken for a real vampire bat!

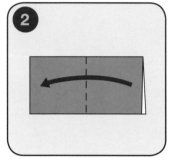

Start with a square, plain side up. Valley fold it in half from top to bottom.

Valley fold the paper in half from right to left.

Lift the top half up along the middle fold-line. Open out the paper and . . .

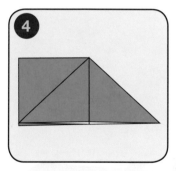

press it down neatly into a triangle.

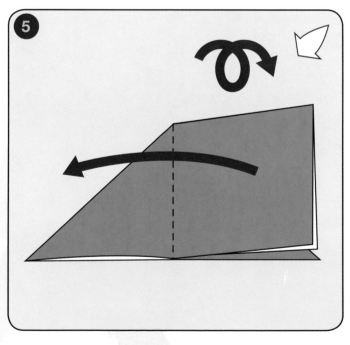

Turn the paper over. Valley fold in half from right to left. Repeat steps 3 and 4 to make a waterbomb base.

6

Holding them together, carefully tear the left-hand sloping edges, to make the ears.

7

From the top point, valley fold the right-hand sloping edge in to meet the middle fold-line.

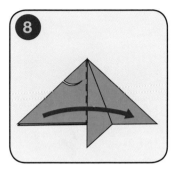

8

Valley fold the left-hand flap of paper over to the right, as . . .

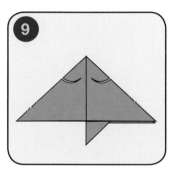

9

though you were turning the page of a book.

10

Turn the paper over. From the top point, valley fold the left-hand sloping edge in to meet the middle fold-line.

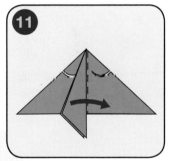

11

Valley fold the left-hand flap of paper over to the right.

 "Aerogami" is the term invented specifically for the art of folding paper planes.

19

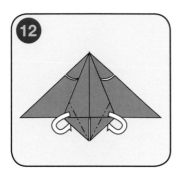

From the bottom points, mountain fold the lower edges behind, so they lie along the middle line. This makes the feet.

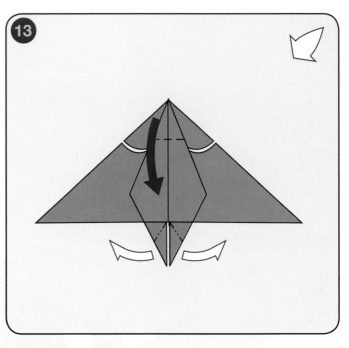

Mountain fold the tips of the feet out to either side. Valley fold the top point down, as shown, to make . . .

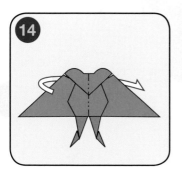

the head and ears appear. Mountain fold the paper in half from left to right.

From just behind the ears, valley fold a little of the front flap's sloping edge over on a slant, as shown. Repeat behind with the back flap.

Valley fold the front flap toward the left, making a wing. Press flat and unfold slightly. Repeat behind with the back flap. To complete, open out the Bat a little and give the tip of each wing a soft downward curve.

To fly, hold the Bat facedown by its feet between the thumb and forefinger and launch it with a gentle push forward. It will glide slowly down to earth.

20

The Helicopter

Difficulty

Here's a flyer you can enjoy without leaving your seat. Just launch the helicopter up toward the overhead compartment, sit back, and see what happens next!

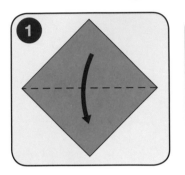

1

Start with a square, printed side up and one corner toward you. Valley fold in half from top to bottom, to make a triangle.

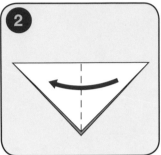

2

Valley fold the triangle in half from right to left.

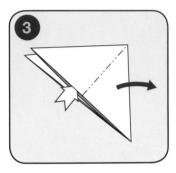

3

Lift the top half up along the middle fold-line. Open out the paper and . . .

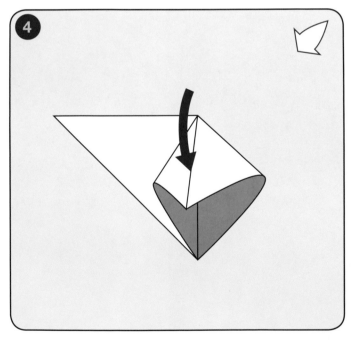

4

press it down neatly . . .

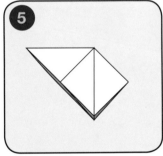

5

into a diamond.

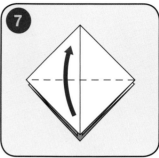

Valley fold the front flap of paper in half from bottom to top.

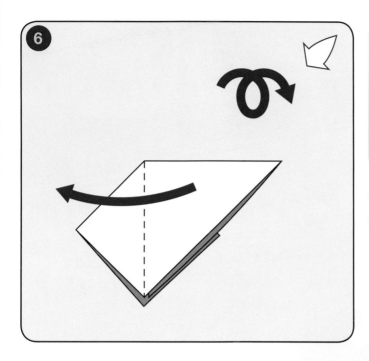

Turn the paper over. Valley fold in half from right to left. Repeat steps 3 to 5 to make a preliminary fold.

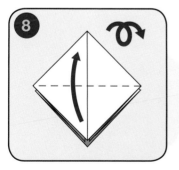

Turn the paper over. Valley fold the front flap of paper in half from bottom to top.

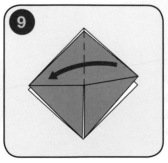

Valley fold the right-hand flap of paper over to the left.

20

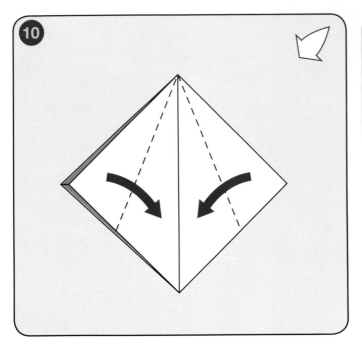

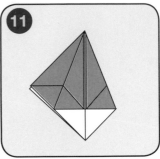

From the top point, valley fold the sloping edges in to meet . . .

the middle fold-line.

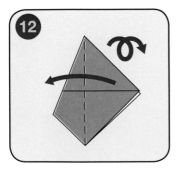

Turn the paper over. Valley fold the right-hand flap of paper over to the left.

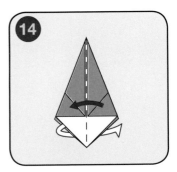

From the top point, valley fold the sloping edges in to meet the middle fold-line.

Valley fold the right-hand flap of paper over to the left, as though turning the page of a book. Repeat behind.

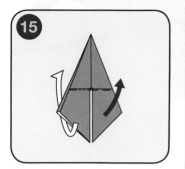

15

Valley fold one bottom point forward, and mountain fold the other one backward slightly. You can make the flyer rotate faster or slower by varying the angle of these folds.

16

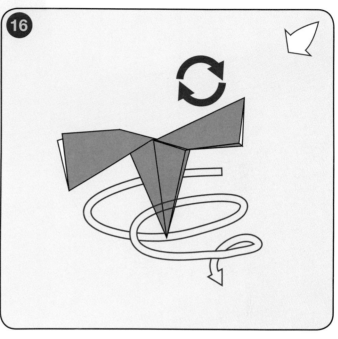

To complete, turn the Helicopter point-downward. To fly, throw it into the air, base end first, and it will turn over, twist around, and pick up speed as it descends.

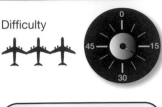

The UFO

Difficulty

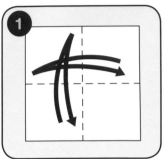

Who knows what part of outer space this flying object might have come from? As the UFO is a little tricky to fold, it's the ideal model to choose for a long flight.

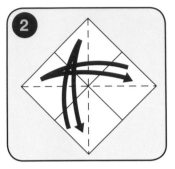

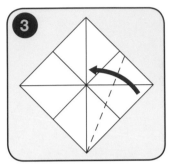

Start with a square, plain side up. Fold and unfold it in half from side to side, and top to bottom.

Turn the square to point toward you. Fold and unfold it in half from corner to corner.

From the bottom corner, valley fold the lower right-hand sloping edge in to meet the middle fold-line.

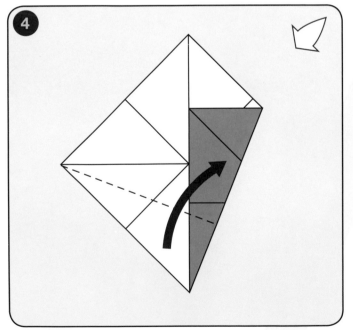

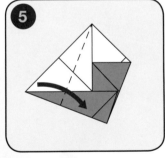

From the top corner, valley fold the upper left-hand sloping edge in to meet the middle fold-line.

From the left-hand corner, valley fold the lower left-hand sloping edge in to meet the middle fold-line.

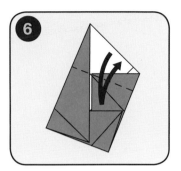

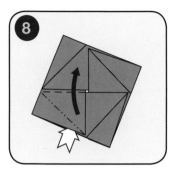

Valley fold the upper right-hand sloping edge over to the point where the inner edges intersect. Press flat and unfold.

Using the fold-lines made in step 6 as a guide, push the upper right-hand sloping edge down inside the model, making a diamond shape.

Valley fold the diamond's lower left-hand side point across the model, as shown; in the process let the paper arrange itself into . . .

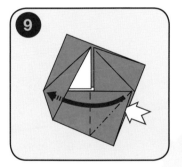

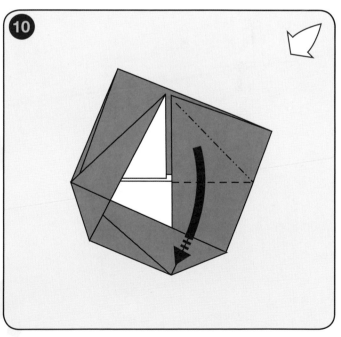

a triangular pointed flap. Repeat step 8 with the diamond's lower right-hand side point, at the same time tucking it underneath the previous one.

Repeat step 9 with the diamond's upper right-hand side point.

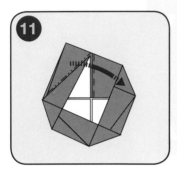 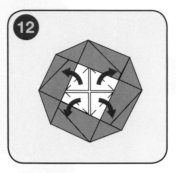 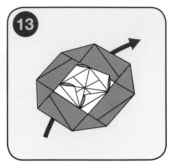

Finally, repeat step 9 with the diamond's upper left-hand side point. In the process, make sure that the points are arranged, as shown in step 12.

To complete, valley fold the four inner corners upright.

To fly, grip one of the UFO's sides between thumb and fingers and launch it spinning into the air by flicking your arm forward.

22

The Hawk

Difficulty

Like its namesake, the Hawk flies swift and sure to its prey. Don't be discouraged by the apparently complex folds in step 8—everything falls into place very easily.

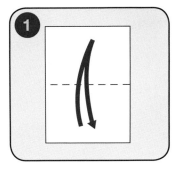

Place the opened-out barfbag lengthways, plain side up. Fold and unfold it in half from bottom to top.

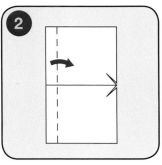

Valley fold the left-hand side over by about an inch. At the right-hand end of the middle fold-line, tear the paper as shown, making two flaps.

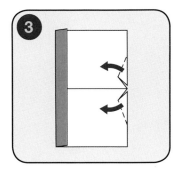

Valley fold each of the right-hand flaps over on a slant.

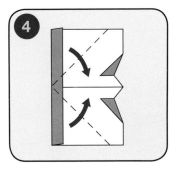

Valley fold the top and bottom left-hand corners in to meet the middle fold-line.

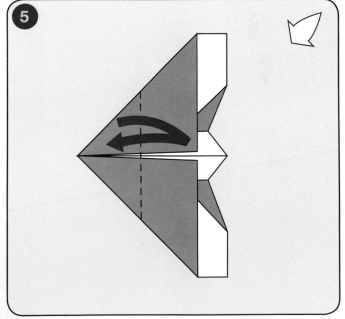

Valley fold the left-hand point over to meet the adjacent vertical edges. Press flat, then unfold.

22

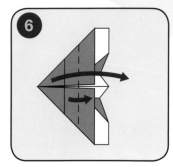

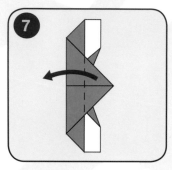

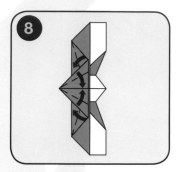

Valley fold the left-hand point over, so that the fold-line made in step 5 lies along the vertical edges.

Valley fold the point over to the left along the fold-line made in step 5.

Working from the left-hand point's tip, bring the top and bottom sloping edges together along the middle fold-line, pressing them . . .

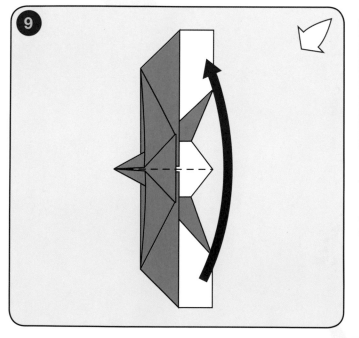

Valley fold the front flap of paper down on a slant, making a wing. Repeat behind with the back flap.

down neatly into collars. Valley fold the paper in half from bottom to top.

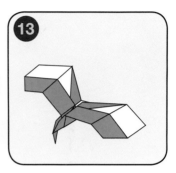

Turn a little of the left-hand point inside out, making the head. Press it neatly down into position, as shown in step 12.

Along a line that starts at the back of the head, valley fold the front wing down on a slant. Repeat with the back wing. Open out the wings into a broad M-shape.

To complete, give the front edge of each wing a soft downward curve. To fly, hold the Hawk by the tip of its tail between the thumb and forefinger and launch it with a gentle push forward.

23 The Shooting Star

Difficulty

This flyer comes with a health and safety warning: It's surprisingly fierce and fast in flight. Unusually, you will need to prepare two barfbag squares of equal size.

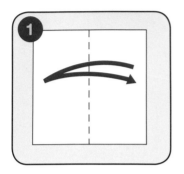

Fold and unfold one square, plain side up, in half vertically.

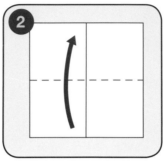

Valley fold the paper in half from bottom to top.

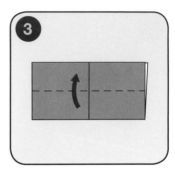

Again, valley fold the paper in half from bottom to top.

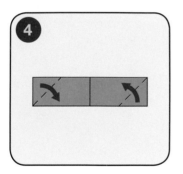

Valley fold the bottom right-hand corner up to meet the top edge. Valley fold the top left-hand corner down to meet the bottom edge.

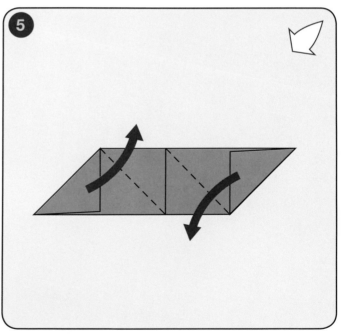

Valley fold the right-hand half of the top edge down and the left-hand half of the bottom edge up, so they lie along . . .

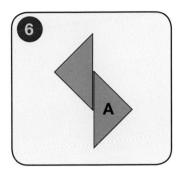

the middle fold-line. Let's call this unit A.

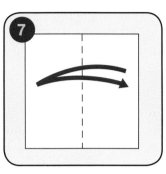

Repeat steps 1 to 3 with the second barfbag square you prepared.

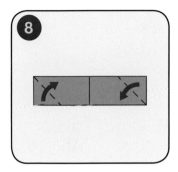

Valley fold the top right-hand corner down to meet the bottom edge. Valley fold the bottom left-hand corner up to meet the top edge.

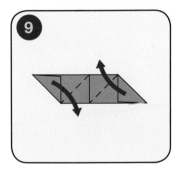

Valley fold the right-hand half of the bottom edge up and the left-hand half of the top edge down, so they lie . . .

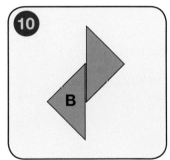

along the middle fold-line. Let's call this unit B.

 In 2008, a Japanese team created a heatproof paper plane to be launched from the International Space Station. Critical scientists rate its chances of floating back down to earth as very low indeed!

23

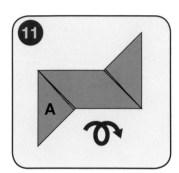

Turn unit A over on to its side, as shown.

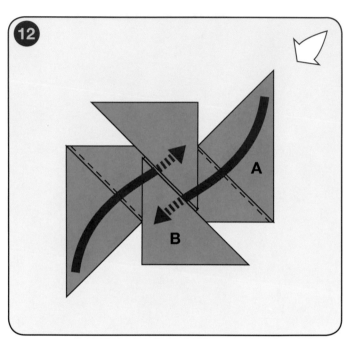

Place unit B on unit A crossways. Tuck the two triangular points of unit A inside unit B with valley folds.

The result should look like this.

Turn both units over. Tuck the two triangular points of unit B inside unit A with valley folds.

Here is the completed flyer.

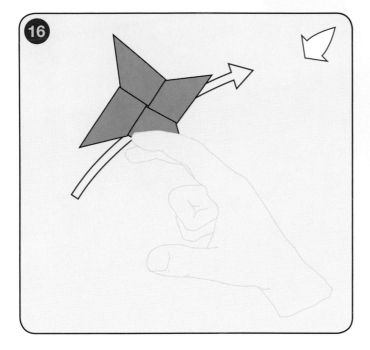

16

To fly, grip one of the Shooting Star's points between the forefinger and middle finger and carefully launch it by flicking your wrist forward. The Shooting Star will spin into the air.

 **24**

The Sycamore Seed

Difficulty

Get your fellow passengers to fold Sycamore Seeds, too—you can hold a competition to see who can keep theirs in the air the longest.

Start with a square, plain side up, and one corner toward you. Fold and unfold it in half from corner to corner to mark the middle fold-lines.

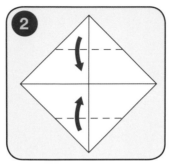

Valley fold the top and bottom corners in to the middle.

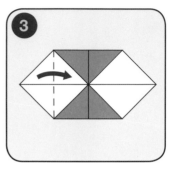

Valley fold the left-hand corner in to the middle.

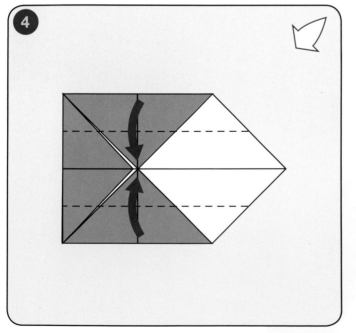

Valley fold the top and bottom edges in to the middle.

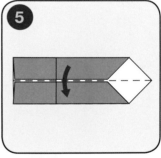

Valley fold the paper in half from top to bottom.

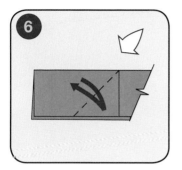

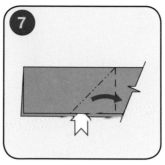

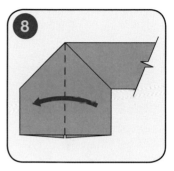

Valley fold the left-hand portion of the top edge down to lie along the vertical fold-line. Press flat, then unfold.

Using the existing fold-lines as a guide, open out the left-hand layers of paper and press them down neatly into . . .

a house-like shape. Valley fold it in half from right to left, making the Sycamore Seed's pod.

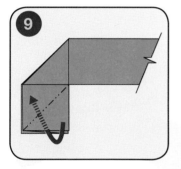

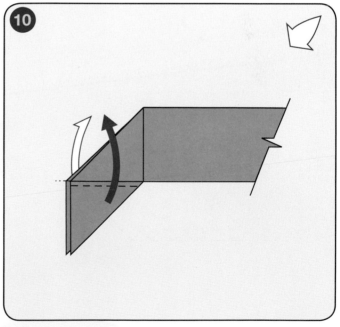

Push the seed pod's lower right-hand corner and its adjoining layers of paper up inside the pod, as shown, making . . .

two triangular flaps. Valley fold one flap up in front and the mountain fold the other behind.

24

Tuck the flaps by their tips into the adjacent sloping pocket. This completes the seed pod.

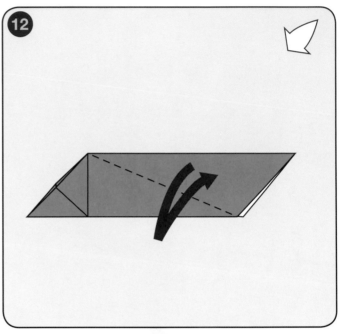

Valley fold the **remaining portion of the top edge** down along a line from top left to **bottom right. Press flat,** then unfold.

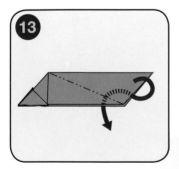

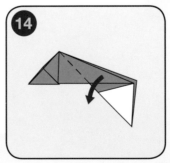

Using the fold-lines made in step 12 as a guide, push the top edge down inside the model, making a flap of paper.

To complete, following the flap's lower sloping edge, valley fold its front layer down, making the flyer's blade.

To fly, hold the Sycamore Seed by its blade between the thumb and forefinger and launch it up into the air.

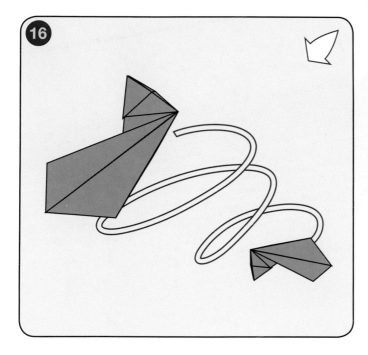

The Sycamore Seed will fall to the ground with a gentle, spinning motion.

 **25**

The Stunt Plane

Difficulty

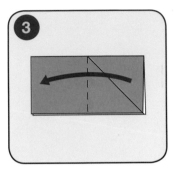

This is probably one of the best flyers ever made. Once you've mastered the steps, you'll have fun discovering the aerobatic moves it can perform.

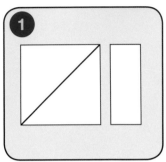

1

Tear your barfbag into a square. Keep the torn-off rectangle: you'll need it for the plane's tail.

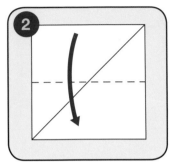

2

To make the body: Valley fold the square in half from top to bottom, plain side up.

3

Valley fold the paper in half from right to left.

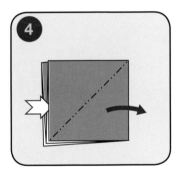

4

Lift the top half up along the middle fold-line. Open out the paper and . . .

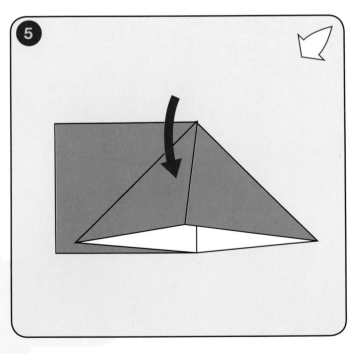

5

press it down neatly into a triangle.

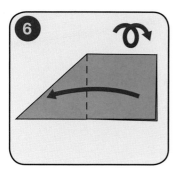

Turn the paper over. Valley fold in half from right to left. Repeat steps 4 and 5 to make a waterbomb base.

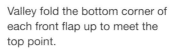

Valley fold the bottom corner of each front flap up to meet the top point.

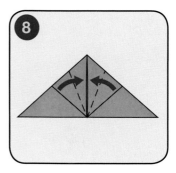

From the middle of the bottom edge, valley fold the two lower sloping edges in to . . .

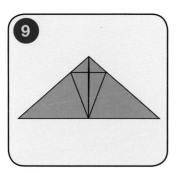

meet the vertical middle line. This completes the body.

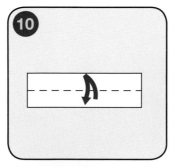

To make the tail: Place the paper rectangle sideways on, plain side up. Fold and unfold it in half from bottom to top.

Using the fold-line made in step 10 as a guide, carefully tear the rectangle of paper in half from side to side. Place one rectangle aside.

25

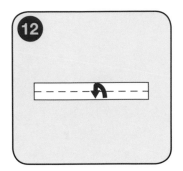

Place the remaining rectangle sideways on, plain side up. Fold and unfold it in half from bottom to top.

Valley fold the rectangle's top and bottom right-hand corners in to meet the middle fold-line. This completes the tail.

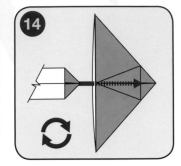

Construction: Insert the tail deep into the body, as shown.

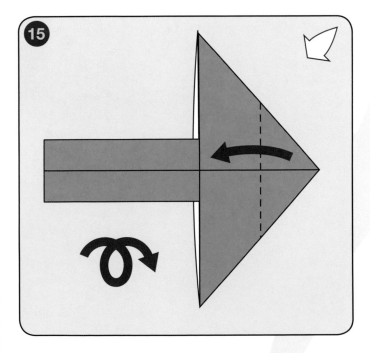

Turn the tail and body over. Valley fold the right-hand point over to meet the middle of the adjacent vertical edge . . .

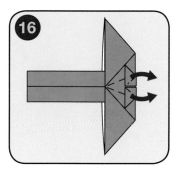

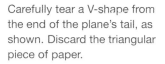

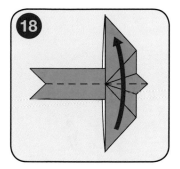

making two pockets appear. Pull them over to the right, so their adjoining sloping edges come to rest along the horizontal middle line. They will look like a bird's beak.

Carefully tear a V-shape from the end of the plane's tail, as shown. Discard the triangular piece of paper.

To complete, valley fold the tail and body in half from bottom to top.

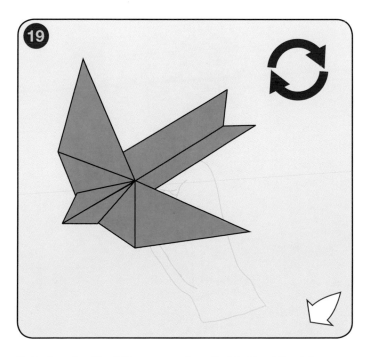

To fly, turn the Stunt Plane around, so that its "beak" points forward and the wings point slightly upward. Hold the plane between thumb and forefinger and launch it gently forward.

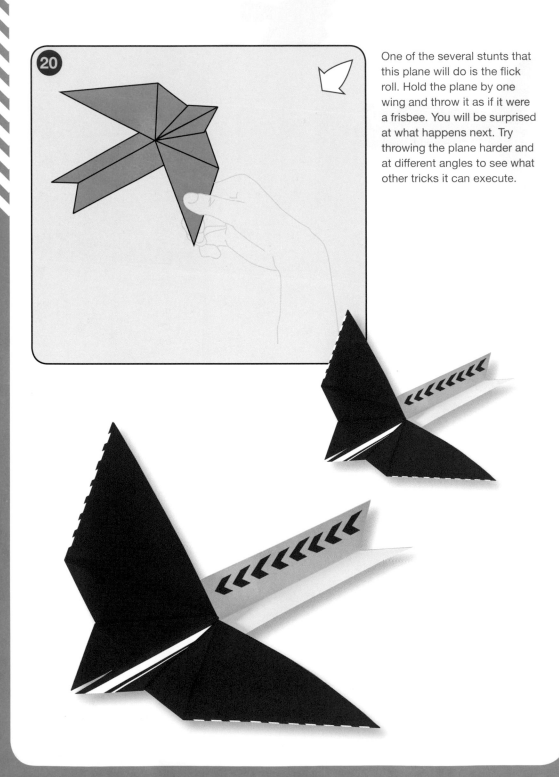

20

One of the several stunts that this plane will do is the flick roll. Hold the plane by one wing and throw it as if it were a frisbee. You will be surprised at what happens next. Try throwing the plane harder and at different angles to see what other tricks it can execute.

26

The Red Admiral

Difficulty

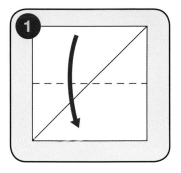

Named after the delightful butterfly commonly seen in Europe and America, this piece doesn't fly, but instead flutters gently when placed on a flat surface.

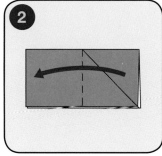

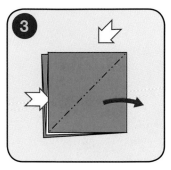

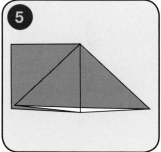

Tear your barfbag into a square. Valley fold it in half from top to bottom, with the plain side on top.

Valley fold the paper in half from right to left.

Lift the top half up along the middle fold-line. Open out the paper . . .

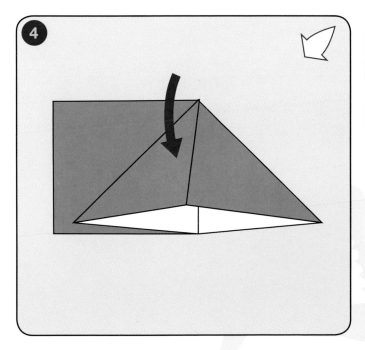

and press it down neatly . . .

into a triangle.

26

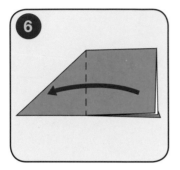

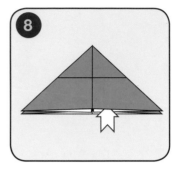

Turn the paper over. Valley fold in half from right to left. Repeat steps 3 to 5 to make a waterbomb base.

Valley fold the top point down to meet the bottom edges. Press flat, then unfold.

Sink the top point. To do this, unfold the paper . . .

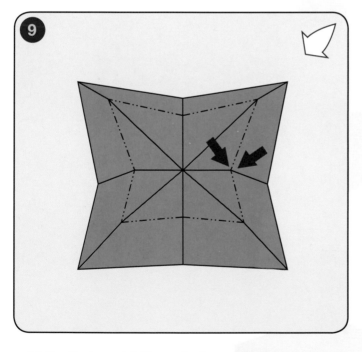

and flatten the top point. Crease the four edges of the inner square into mountain folds.

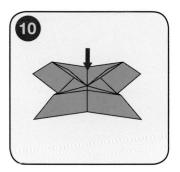

Push down on the middle of the square, at the same time pushing in the sides, so that they collapse toward the middle. Keep on pushing . . .

until the square fully collapses, thereby inverting the top point. inside the waterbomb base.

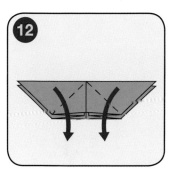

Turn the paper around. Valley fold the front flaps down to . . .

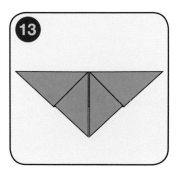

meet the middle fold-line, making the back wings.

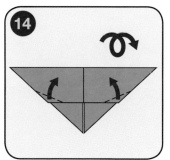

Turn the paper over. Valley fold the two side points of the horizontal edge up on a slight slant.

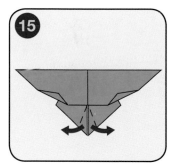

Valley fold the bottom points out to either side on a slant.

The longest time a paper plane has stayed in the air is over twenty-seven seconds. If you count the seconds out, you'll realize just how impressive this record is!

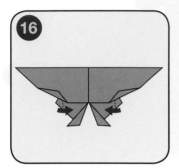

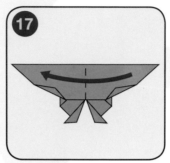

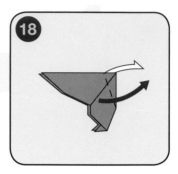

Valley fold the right- and left-hand side points in on a slight slant.

Valley fold the paper in half from right to left.

Valley fold the front flap of paper over to the right on a slant, as shown. Repeat behind with the back flap.

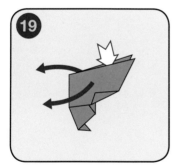

Place the Butterfly on a flat surface and lightly tap its body as shown. The wings will flutter up and down.

To complete, lift the wings up, so that they are at right angles to the body.

 **27**

The Flapping Crane

Difficulty

This is the grandfather of all traditional flying objects, and everyone will want one. So be ready with a large number of barfbag squares to meet those requests.

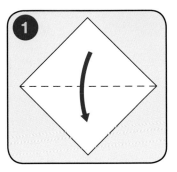

Start with a square, plain side up, and one corner toward you. Valley fold it in half from top to bottom, to make a triangle.

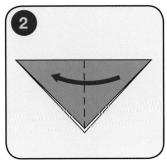

Valley fold the triangle in half from right to left.

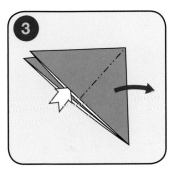

Lift the top half up along the middle fold-line. Open out the paper . . .

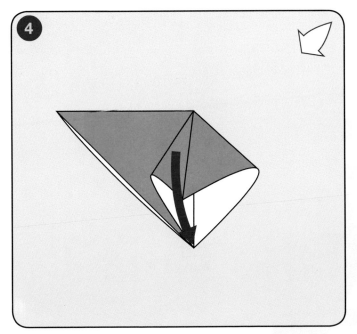

and press it down neatly . . .

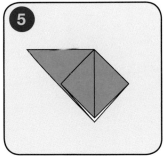

into a diamond.

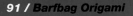

27

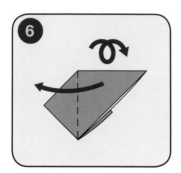

Turn the paper over. Valley fold it in half from right to left. Repeat steps 3 to 5 to make a preliminary fold.

From the bottom point, valley fold the lower (open) sloping edges in to meet the middle fold-line. Press flat, then unfold.

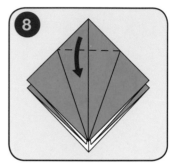

Valley fold the top point down along a horizontal line that runs between the top of the sloping fold-lines, as shown.

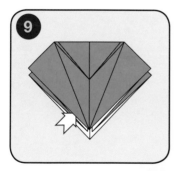

Pinch and lift up the front **flap** of paper.

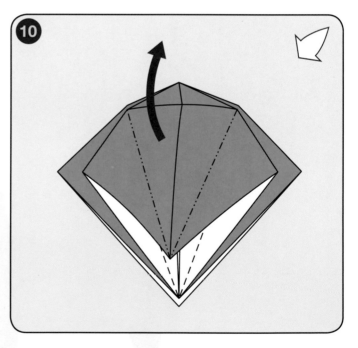

Continue to lift up the flap . . .

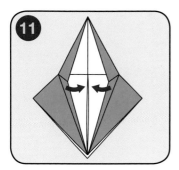

so that its edges meet in the middle.

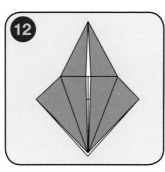

Press the paper flat, so that it becomes diamond shaped.

Turn the paper over. Repeat steps 7 to 12 to make a bird base.

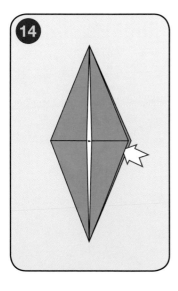

Open out the right-hand layers of paper slightly . . .

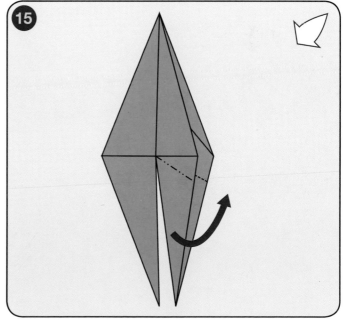

and pull the adjoining bottom point up . . .

27

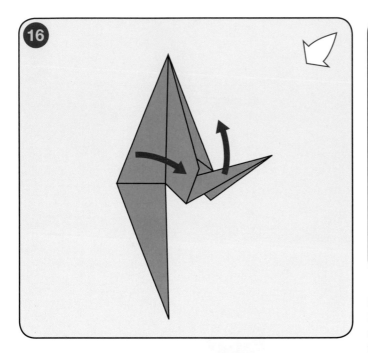

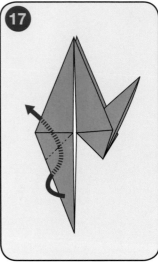

inside itself. When the point is in the right **position**, as shown in step 17, press it flat to make the neck.

Repeat steps 14 to 16 with the left-hand layers of paper and adjoining **bottom** point. When the **point is in the right position, as shown in** step 18, press it flat, this **time to make the tail.**

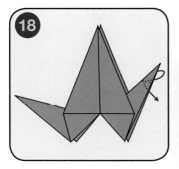

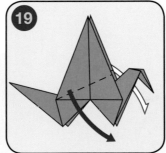

Push the neck's tip down inside itself, making the bird's head.

To complete the bird, gently curve the wings in the direction of the head.

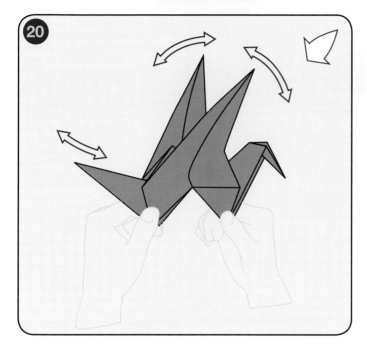

To fly, hold the chest with one hand and pull the Flapping Crane's tail gently back and forth with the other to make the wings flap.

Links page

If you have enjoyed folding the various projects in *Barfbag Origami,* then it's recommended that you get in touch with the following origami organizations. They offer a wide range of paperfolding materials, books, private publications, and information on many international origami associations.

OrigamiUSA
15 West 77th Street
New York
New York 10024-5192
USA
www.origami-usa.org

The Membership Secretary
British Origami Society
2A The Chestnuts
Countesthorpe
Leicestershire LE8 5TL
England
www.britishorigami.org.uk

The Internet is a great resource for finding information on origami and paper planes. Below are some favorites, all of which have links to other related sites.

Joseph Wu's Origami
A treasure trove of information on origami.
www.origami.as/home.html

Alex's Paper Planes
An award-winning paper airplane site.
www.paperairplanes.co.uk

Paper Airplanes and more
Homepage for world record paper airplanes.
www.paperplane.org

Paper Airplanes
This site presents a list of links to Web pages on paper airplanes.
www.cdli.ca/CITE/paper.htm

Acknowledgements
Chris Marks, project consultant, would like to thank the following:
Tomomi Akashi, Ben Childs, Tetsuo Okuyama, and Nigel Stevens for sharing their paper creations. A special thank you to James Richardson and his family for testing the instructions and reviewing the text. Finally I would like to express my gratitude to the Paperwasp production team. It has been a pleasure to work with you all.

About the Author
Chris Marks was born in 1960 and grew up in the northeast of England. Throughout a varied career that has included advertising, graphic design, paper engineering, teaching English as a foreign language, and writing, he has consistently been experimenting with folded paper designs that fly. He has traveled extensively in South America and Asia, and now lives with his wife, family, and two Siamese cats on the English Riviera.